B·I·B·L·E W·O·R·L·D

WIND AND FIRE
Spreading the Message of Jesus

WORLD RELIEF
316 Maynard Ave. South-Suite 103
Seattle, WA 98104-2719

For Michael Lush

First published in the United States of America in 1995 by Thomas Nelson, Inc., Publishers, Nashville, Tennessee, and distributed in Canada by Word Communications, Ltd., Richmond, British Columbia.

Text by John Drane

Published by
Lion Publishing plc
Sandy Lane West, Oxford, England
ISBN 0-7459-2179-5
Albatross Books Pty Ltd
PO Box 320, Sutherland, NSW 2232, Australia
ISBN 0-7324-0549-1

First edition 1995

Contributors to this volume
John Drane is Director of the Center for the Study of Christianity and Contemporary Society at the University of Stirling and the author of several highly-acclaimed books on the Bible and its history written in a way that young people can understand and enjoy.

Alan Millard, Rankin Professor of Hebrew and Ancient Semitic Languages at Liverpool University, is the consultant for the illustrations in this book, and all the books in the series.

Acknowledgments
All photographs are copyright © Lion Publishing, except the following:
Sonia Halliday: 3 (left), 10 (above left), 14 (above right)
Michael Holford: 14 (below right)
Oxford Scientific Films © Gordon A. Maclean: 18 (left)
Clifford Shirley: 19 (right)
Lois Rock: 17 (below left)
Zefa: 17 (above left, above right)

The following Lion Publishing photographs appear by courtesy of:
the British Museum: 11 (above left)
the Eretz Israel Museum, Tel Aviv: 15 (below left), 20 (above left)

Illustrations, copyright © Lion Publishing, by:
Jeffrey Burn: 11 (below left), 16
Chris Molan: 1, 2, 3, 4, 5, 6, 7, 8, 9, 10, 11, 12, 13, 14, 15, 16 (left), 17, 18, 19, 20

Maps, copyright © Lion Publishing, by:
Oxford Illustrators Ltd: 1 (left and center), 2, 4, 5, 6, 8, 13, 20

Bible quotations are taken from the *Good News Bible*, copyright © American Bible Society, New York, 1966, 1971 and 4th edition 1976, published by the Bible Societies/HarperCollins, with permission.

Story text is based on material from *The Lion Children's Bible*, by Pat Alexander.

ISBN 0-7852-7905-9

Printed and bound in Malaysia

1 2 3 4 5—

B·I·B·L·E WORLD

WIND AND FIRE

SPREADING THE MESSAGE OF JESUS

John Drane

OLIVER NELSON

THOMAS NELSON PUBLISHERS
Nashville • Atlanta • London • Vancouver

Contents

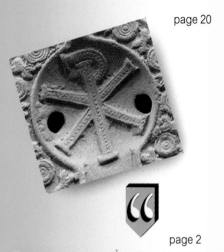

page 20

page 2

page 13

page 17

page 11

page 14

page 15

page 16

page 9

page 5

1 Small Beginnings

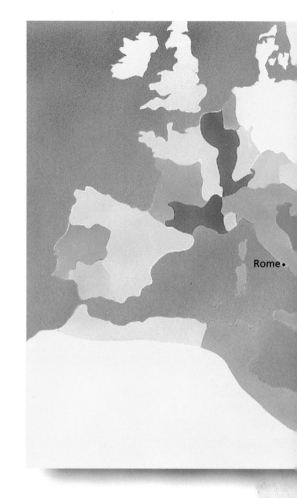

It is almost 2,000 years since the time when Jesus lived, but millions of people all over the world today still follow His teachings. These people are called Christians. One out of every three people in the world is a Christian. That means there are about two billion of them! Any group of Christians meeting together regularly is called a church, and there are churches in just about every country of the world.

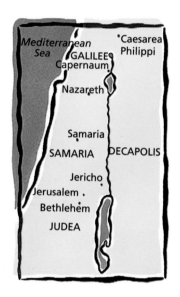

Where Jesus lived
Jesus worked and lived in Palestine—a tiny country on the eastern edge of the Roman Empire. When He was put to death in Jerusalem, no one would have guessed how far the news about Him would spread.

The start of the church

The church began in a small way. Jesus Himself lived in a small village in Palestine, on the very edge of the Roman Empire. He never traveled far, and His followers, or "disciples," were very ordinary people. By the end of Jesus' life there were only a few hundred disciples, almost all of them living in the region of Galilee where Jesus' own home had been.

Twenty or thirty years later, however, groups of Jesus' followers could be found in every major city of the Empire, including Rome itself.

The way the church grew during this period is one of the most exciting stories in the whole of history. Jesus' followers did not have an easy time. Some were put into prison, and even put to death. But Jesus had promised that wherever they went, they would know that God was with them. That gave them great confidence and courage, because they knew they could trust Jesus.

The Roman Empire
From its almost unnoticed beginnings in Palestine, Christianity spread rapidly to many different provinces. This map shows the different provinces in the Empire around A.D.100.

Athens•

• Antioch

Mediterranean Sea

Jerusalem •

Spreading the message

Life was tough for the first followers of Jesus, the first Christians. Jesus Himself had sent them out to share His message with other people. But they faced a real challenge! The first Christians were neither rich nor famous; few of them were well educated, and they had no big organization to back them up.

However, some things about the Roman Empire helped them spread their news:

● **All the big cities were linked.** They were linked to one another and to Rome, by a great network of roads and sea routes. This made it easy for Christians to travel with their message. People who became Christians in the cities often took the message to more remote towns and villages.

● **People everywhere could understand Greek.** It was the international language of the Roman Empire. That made communication a lot easier!

● **There were communities of Jewish people living all over the Empire.** In fact, there were more Jewish people living outside Palestine than in it! They met every week in their synagogues, to worship God and to study their ancient Scriptures. The Christians believed that Jesus was the Messiah of whom these Scriptures spoke. Not surprisingly, Jewish people were very interested to hear what the Christians had to say about Jesus.

● **Many people were looking for something to believe in.** The philosophers of Greece and Italy had asked a lot of hard questions about Greek and Roman religion. As a result, many ordinary people no longer believed in the old gods. But the teachings of the philosophers were complex and hard to understand. People were looking for something they could believe in, and they welcomed new religious teachers from other parts of the Empire.

◄ **Philip and the Ethiopian**
The first Christians took every opportunity to tell people about Jesus. The Bible book known as Acts describes how a Christian named Philip struck up a conversation with an important government official from Ethiopia as they traveled along the same road. Philip was invited into the man's carriage—and soon the Ethiopian was asking to be baptized as a sign that he was now a Christian.

2 Wind and Fire

When Jesus was crucified, His followers had no idea what they should do next.

It was one of Jesus' closest disciples, Judas, who had betrayed Him to the authorities. He was so ashamed of himself that he committed suicide.

The other disciples had seen Jesus alive again on several occasions. But one day He said a final farewell. Before He left, Jesus said that they would know when they had God's power to tell others the news about Him: They would receive God's Spirit. Meanwhile, although they still believed that Jesus was the Messiah and Son of God, they were terrified.

It was on the day of Pentecost, a Jewish festival, that everything changed.

Pentecost

Jesus was crucified during the Jewish religious festival of Passover. Pentecost was another festival that came fifty days later. It was a time for giving thanks to God for the grain harvest. Pilgrims traveled from all over the world to celebrate these events in the temple at Jerusalem.

A SPECIAL PENTECOST

Jesus' friends were together in a house in Jerusalem. Suddenly it felt as if a strong wind was blowing, and something looking like flames of fire touched each person. Jesus had promised to send God's Spirit—and now the Spirit had arrived! The disciples were amazed to find they were able to speak in languages they had never learned. They felt completely different too. Before, they had been timid and afraid, not sure they could go on following Jesus. Now they knew for certain that all He had told them was true, and they wanted to go out and share the good news with everyone they met.

It was Pentecost, an important religious festival, and Jerusalem was crowded with visitors from all over the world. When these visitors heard what had happened—in their own languages, spoken by Jesus' followers—

they knew something extraordinary was taking place.

"This is a really special day," said Peter. "Do you remember what the prophet Joel wrote many centuries ago, how God would give the Holy Spirit to women and men everywhere?"

Most of the people did. They had heard the ancient Scriptures read in worship at the synagogue.

"Well," said Peter, "today the Spirit has come." As he spoke of what Jesus had said and done, and of His death and resurrection, many of those who heard wanted to know more.

"Change your way of life and believe in Jesus," Peter said.

And three thousand of them became Christians there and then.

▶ **Pilgrims from many places**
Pilgrims from all the places shown here heard Peter's message about Jesus at Pentecost. They included Gentiles who followed the Jewish religion as well as people from Jewish families. They would have spread the news about Jesus when they returned home—west as far as Rome, and east to regions beyond this map as shown by the arrows.

The birthday of the church

The day of Pentecost was the day when the church was born. Before that, the only followers of Jesus were people who had known Him in person. From that day on, however, people who had never met or seen Jesus would believe in Him as God's Son and Messiah.

Following Jesus did not change only what they thought about Him. It also affected the way they acted toward others. Some of these new Christians were very rich, and some were poor. They all sold what they owned and pooled the money so that they could all share it.

3 Danger Ahead

In the days following Peter's amazing speech to the crowd, the number of new Christians kept on growing. These people met one another every day: to pray, to praise God, and to enjoy being together. Sometimes they met in one another's homes. At other times they met in the Jewish temple. They even worshiped in the street. Wherever they were, their thoughts were of Jesus.

Hard questions

The Jewish religious leaders had mixed feelings about these followers of Jesus. They could see that people's lives were being changed because of their belief in Jesus. Some were even being healed in the name of Jesus! But the Jewish leaders feared that they were losing the respect of their people.

Peter and John were arrested and called before the Jewish Council to explain themselves. They were warned not to speak openly of Jesus, but no sooner had they been set free than they were back in the streets again talking of Him. It seemed as if nothing would stop them—and more people were joining them all the time.

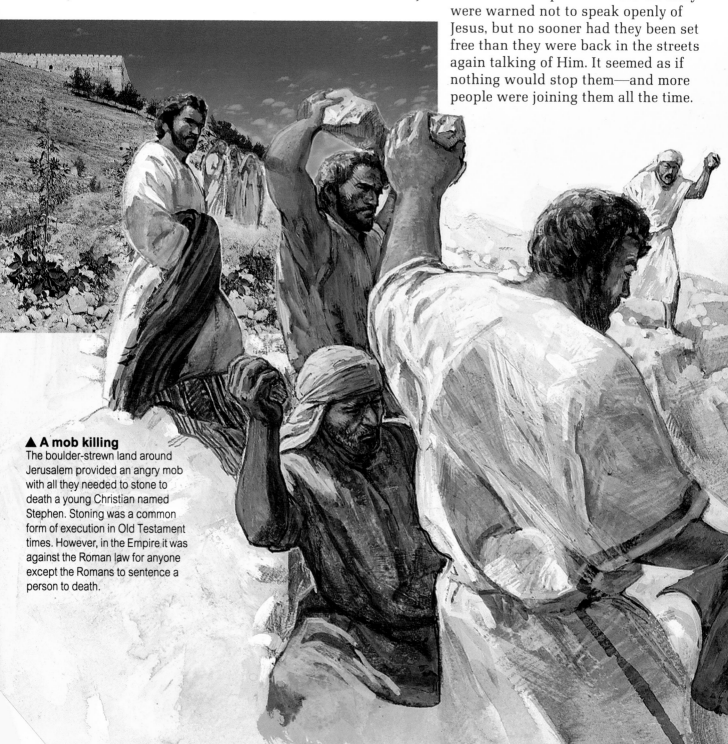

▲ **A mob killing**
The boulder-strewn land around Jerusalem provided an angry mob with all they needed to stone to death a young Christian named Stephen. Stoning was a common form of execution in Old Testament times. However, in the Empire it was against the Roman law for anyone except the Romans to sentence a person to death.

A CHRISTIAN IS KILLED

As the number of Christians grew, new leaders were appointed. After praying and asking for God's guidance, the original leaders chose seven others. One was a young man called Stephen. He was not one of Jesus' first disciples, but he really trusted God and believed Jesus was the Messiah.

That made him unpopular with some people, and they began to complain about him.

"We heard this man speaking against the Jewish law and against God," they claimed.

Stephen was put on trial before the Jewish Council. He spoke about the history of the Jewish nation, and of how even God's own people disobeyed God's laws.

"Now," Stephen said, "you have done something even worse: You have allowed God's own Son, Jesus, to be put to death. But He is still alive: In fact, I can see Him now, beside God in heaven!"

This made people so angry that Stephen was stoned to death. He became the first Christian martyr—he was ready to die rather than give up his faith in Jesus. But there were Jewish leaders who did not oppose the Christians. A rabbi called Gamaliel gave the Council wise advice:

"If what these people are saying is false, then no one is going to believe them. But if it is really true, then by opposing them we may find ourselves fighting against God."

Seven deacons

In the first days, the leaders of the church were those who had been Jesus' closest followers when He was alive. As the church in Jerusalem kept growing, they chose seven helpers, sometimes called "deacons." Their job was to serve other Christians—that is what the Greek word *diakonia* means. As well as Stephen, there was Philip, who took the message about Jesus to an Ethiopian official traveling from Jerusalem and who later became a leader in the church at Caesarea, together with Prochorus, Nicanor, Timon, Parmenas, and Nicolas. We don't know anything about these others, except that Nicolas was from Antioch, and was not Jewish by birth.

4 The Persecutor

After Stephen's death, many Christians were so afraid for their own safety that they left Jerusalem for Damascus in Syria. But one of their enemies, a young man named Saul, was determined they should not escape so easily.

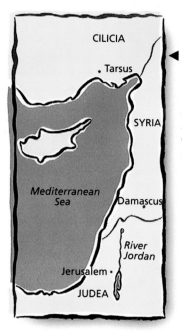

◀ Places in Saul's early life
Saul was born in Tarsus, studied in Jerusalem, and met Jesus in a dramatic way on the road to Damascus.

Saul

Saul was a young Jew who had studied the Hebrew Scriptures carefully. He was convinced that what the Christians were claiming must be wrong. How could Jesus possibly be the Messiah, he asked, when everyone knew He had been crucified by the Romans?

When Stephen was put to death, Saul had stood on the edge of the crowd, looking after the coats of those who threw the stones that killed him.

When Saul heard that the Christians were fleeing to Damascus, he asked the authorities for permission to go after them, arrest them, and put them in prison.

On the road to Damascus, something happened that made him change his mind.

ON THE ROAD TO DAMASCUS

As Saul traveled along the road, a strange thing happened. The sun was shining brightly anyway. But the light seemed to keep on getting brighter and brighter. It became so bright it was blinding him. Saul stumbled and fell in the dazzling light. Then he heard someone call his name.

"Saul! Why are you trying to kill Me?"

"What do You mean?" asked Saul. "And who are You, anyway?"

"I am Jesus," the voice said. "I am really alive, as those Christians say. By hunting them you are attacking Me. Go on to Damascus, and when you

get there someone will tell you what to do next."

Saul's companions knew something strange had happened, as Saul could no longer see. Then, as they were leading him by the hand into Damascus, a Christian called Ananias also received a message from God in a vision, telling him to visit Saul and restore his sight.

Ananias knew all about Saul. He was afraid this was some kind of trap, and that he would be arrested. But God reassured him:

"Saul is special. I have called him to follow Jesus and take the good news to the whole world."

When Saul's sight was restored, he was a different person. Instead of putting the Christians in jail, he went straight to the Jewish synagogue to speak about Jesus.

Saul and his family

Like many Jewish people, Saul was not a native of Palestine. He was born in Tarsus, an important city in Cilicia, which is in the south of present-day Turkey. His parents sent him to Jerusalem to learn about the traditions of his people. His family must have been quite rich, as Saul could afford to travel all over the Empire and make contact with people in high places.

Roman citizens

Saul was also a Roman citizen. Not everyone in the Empire was a citizen. It was a special privilege, and Saul's family must have been given the honor long before he was born. Many residents of Tarsus were made Roman citizens after they helped a Roman general, Pompey, in 64 B.C. Saul's father or grandfather may have been one of them. No one knows how people proved their citizenship, but perhaps they had some kind of certificate or medallion.

Did you know?

Saul is generally called Paul in the New Testament. His family gave him the Hebrew name Saul, after Israel's first king. But, as a Christian, most of his life was spent among non-Jewish people, which is why he mostly used the Latin form of his name —Paul.

5 Peter Leads the Way

Peter was one of Jesus' first disciples, and after his dramatic speech in Jerusalem on the day of Pentecost, he began traveling to other places, telling people about Jesus.

One day, when he was in the ancient city of Joppa, he had a strange dream which began to change his idea of what kind of people could be Christians.

As a result, Peter led the way in taking the message to all people, regardless of their race. As Jesus had said, His message was for everyone.

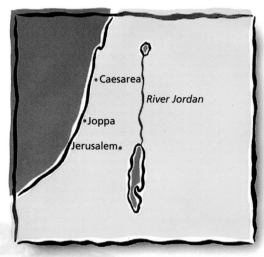

▲ **Peter's travels**
Peter's early travels took him only as far as the coast of Palestine. However, taking the news about Jesus to a Gentile such as Cornelius marked a real breakthrough.

PETER'S DREAM

Peter had traveled to Joppa, and was staying in the house of Simon the leatherworker. One day, about noon, he went up onto the flat roof of the house, overlooking the sea, so that he could spend some time praying before having a meal. While he was there, he had a special kind of dream.

In this dream, he saw a big sheet being lowered like a stretcher. On it were all sorts of birds and animals.

"Get up, Peter," said a voice. "Kill some of them and have a feast."

"I can't do that," replied Peter. "God's law forbids Jewish people to eat this kind of food."

"Don't say that," said the voice, "because God has said they are all fit to eat."

This happened three times, and then Peter woke up. What could it possibly mean?

Soon afterward, three messengers arrived. They had been sent by an officer in the Roman army who was stationed at nearby Caesarea. His name was Cornelius.

"Cornelius loves God and would like to hear about Jesus," they said. But Peter wasn't sure. Up to now, most Christians had been Jewish people. The Jews had many strict laws about mixing with people of other races. They called them "Gentiles," and Cornelius was certainly one of them —Roman, in fact, and a soldier. The Jews had suffered a lot from the Roman army. Why should Peter take the message of Jesus to someone like that?

Then he remembered the dream. Maybe God was trying to tell him something. So he accepted the invitation and went to Cornelius's home.

When Cornelius and his friends heard what Peter had to say about Jesus, they believed him and were baptized. So Peter knew that Gentiles could be Christians too.

Did you know?

Caesarea was a magnificent sea port, built by King Herod the Great just a few years before Jesus was born. Its grand buildings were designed by Greek and Roman architects. Many Romans lived there, because it reminded them of the great cities of Italy and Greece. But there were Jewish people there too. It was the home of Philip, who was appointed one of the church's first seven deacons, along with Stephen. Philip may have been the first Christian to take the message of Jesus to people in the city.

▲ Roman theater
The great amphitheater at Caesarea was a place where Roman-style entertainments could be put on for the many Romans who lived in the city.

God-fearers

In the time of the Roman Empire, there were many Jewish communities with synagogues outside Palestine, and many non-Jews came on the Sabbath. Some simply enjoyed the prayer and Scripture teaching. Others believed in the God the Jewish Scriptures described as the one true God. They were known as "God-fearers." The Roman officer named Cornelius who became a follower of Jesus when he heard Peter speak of Him was one of these.

Still others wanted to be as fully Jewish as they could, and they accepted all the laws of the Jewish Scriptures. These people were called "proselytes."

◀ Dreaming on the rooftops
The flat roofs of the houses in Palestine were often used as extra living space. Sometimes cloth awnings were put up to provide shade . . . and perhaps the awning became part of Peter's special dream.

6 A Dangerous Journey

Some years had passed since Saul—now more usually known as Paul—became a Christian. The church at Antioch in Syria was now one of the largest anywhere. Paul was living there, with his friend Barnabas, teaching people about the Christian faith. However, there was other work to be done.

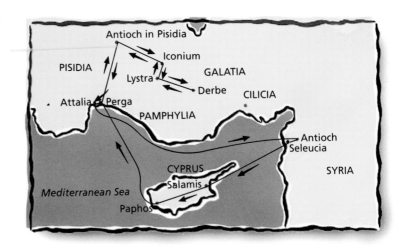

▶Paul begins his travels
Paul's first major journey to tell people about Jesus took him and his companion, Barnabas, to Cyprus and then by sea and land to the important towns in Asia Minor—present-day Turkey.

SPECIAL INSTRUCTIONS

One day the Christians in Antioch were praying. Some of them were prophets and they brought a message they knew was from God. "I need Barnabas and Paul for a special job. They must go to the people who still know nothing about Jesus."

The church gave them its blessing, and sent them off. They went first to Cyprus, where Barnabas had been born. The Roman governor of the island, Sergius Paulus, made them welcome. He listened to all they had to say, and became a follower of Jesus himself. It was a good beginning.

Another sea voyage took them to Turkey.

There, they traveled overland—mostly on foot—from town to town.

They always went to the synagogues first, to tell the Jews that Jesus was the Messiah promised in their Scriptures. But they also spoke to Gentiles.

Not everyone liked their message. Paul and Barnabas stirred up trouble, and they had some narrow escapes.

But in every town some people were eager to listen and put their trust in Jesus. Paul and Barnabas spent some time teaching them and then chose leaders for each new Christian group before they moved on.

A working preacher

No one was paying Paul to be a full-time preacher. Jewish religious teachers always took a job to support themselves, and Paul did the same. He was a tent-maker. In those days, tents were made of leather, and Paul would set up a stall in the marketplace where he would make and repair all kinds of leather goods.

This was a good way to get to know people in a strange town. There were no church buildings at this time, and in any case Paul knew that many people would never dream of going to a religious meeting. If people spent their time in the streets or the market, then that was where he would go to speak to them about Jesus.

▶ **Meeting people where they are**
Paul was as happy talking to people about Jesus in a busy marketplace as he was in the synagogue.

Jews and Gentiles

The new Christians whom Barnabas and Paul left behind in each place they visited were keen to follow Jesus, but they still had a lot to learn about their new faith. As Paul and Barnabas headed back home, other Christians visited these new churches and taught them.

However, what they said soon created problems. They claimed that since Jesus was the Jewish Messiah, only Jewish people could be Christians. If non-Jews—Gentiles—wanted to follow Jesus, they would need to accept the Jewish faith first.

When Paul heard this, he wrote an urgent letter to the new Christians in Galatia. This is in the New Testament, so anyone can read what Paul said:

 It is through faith that you are God's children. When you were baptized, you became one with Jesus—each of you. So there is no difference between Jews and Gentiles, between slaves and free people, between men and women.

◀ **Setting out**
Paul and Barnabas left Antioch in Syria and sailed from the nearby port of Seleucia. They probably traveled on one of the Roman merchant ships.

7 Jews and Gentiles

The church at Antioch was a good church, and its people were kind and caring. When they heard there was a famine in Jerusalem, they sent food to the Christians there. The Christians in Jerusalem were grateful for this help. But they were not happy about other things that were happening in Antioch. In particular they were not happy about the way Gentile Christians lived their lives.

Jewish and Gentile Christians

At the start, most Christians were Jews. There were many customs that the Jews had been brought up to follow. Was it necessary to follow these customs to be a Christian? As the church grew, things changed rapidly, and that raised some tricky questions. There seemed to be no easy answer. The church in Antioch included many Gentile Christians. They decided to send Paul and Barnabas to Jerusalem to sort the problems out.

▼ Problems at a party

A party is no fun if half the guests can't eat the food that is served. In the early days of the church, it was hard for Jewish and Gentile Christians to share a meal together. Jewish people thought it was wrong to eat food not prepared according to the Jewish law. But Gentile Christians found it hard to believe those laws were important. It was not easy for them to learn to love one another as fellow believers in Jesus and members of God's family. Both sides had to be willing to change the way they behaved.

Paul and the big question

Paul was well educated, and he knew the Hebrew Scriptures very well. As a leading figure in the growing church he now found he had to explain those Scriptures to help both Jewish and Gentile Christians agree on what they meant. These are some of the points he made.

● **The Hebrew Scriptures talked about God's special people and the laws they must obey.** Centuries before, God had given great promises to Abraham, the ancestor of the whole Jewish nation. From then on the Jews always thought of themselves as God's special people. Over the years, God had also given them laws which were different from those of other nations. Paul had been raised to keep all those laws himself.

● **But anyone who believed in God's promised Messiah, Jesus, was now part of God's special people.** One of the promises was to send a Messiah. Paul, like all the Christians, believed that Jesus was the promised Messiah. That meant anyone who followed Jesus would be a member of God's special people.

● **Did that mean everyone who wanted to follow Jesus should also keep all the old laws?** That was what the church in Jerusalem was asking, and it was a good question. Paul took a fresh look at the ancient Scriptures. He read the story of Abraham carefully. He found that Abraham himself wasn't required to keep any special rules before God's promise to him could come true. The only thing he did was to believe what God was saying!

● **Surely, then, Paul said, there must be only one thing that makes a person a Christian: believing what Jesus said.** If Abraham never kept any complicated rules, then why should Gentiles, who just wanted to follow Jesus?

Paul's explanation sounded simple enough, but it took the young church a long time before people finally agreed on the answers to all these questions.

The meeting in Jerusalem

The people who met in Jerusalem to sort out the problems between Jewish and Gentile Christians included some of the leading figures in the church: Peter, the disciple Jesus chose to start the church; James, Jesus' brother; Paul, and Barnabas. They agreed not to burden Gentile Christians with Jewish laws. But they were still uneasy, and they wondered if the Gentile Christians would be willing to give up some of the things that Jews found particularly hard to live with, such as eating meat that hadn't been prepared in the Jewish way. The people from Antioch agreed it seemed a reasonable idea, and took that message back to their own home church. It was a great encouragement to the church in Antioch to know that Gentile Christians would not be asked to keep all the Jewish laws.

8 A New Adventure

Barnabas and Paul had returned from Jerusalem to Antioch. The problem of Jewish and Gentile Christians had been sorted out for the moment, and the two men were eager to take the message of Jesus to new places. Barnabas took his cousin Mark to Cyprus. Paul took Silas with him when he revisited the new Christians in south Galatia. They were later joined by a young man named Timothy. But where should they go next?

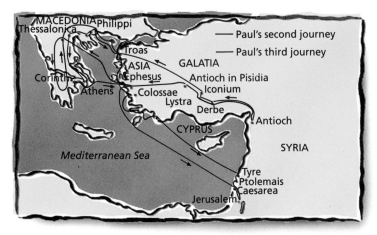

▲ More journeys of Paul
On his second and third big trips telling people about Jesus, Paul went to Macedonia—in the north of present-day Greece.

Paul visits Europe

From Galatia, the obvious place to go was the Roman province of Asia. But in a special kind of dream, Paul saw a Macedonian who said, "We need you to come over here and help us." At the port of Troas they were joined by an enthusiastic Gentile Christian named Luke. Then they all sailed across to Philippi, a Roman colony in Macedonia.

There were not enough Jews there to have their own synagogue—that required at least ten men. But on the Jewish Sabbath, a few people met by the river-bank to pray and read their Scriptures. They listened to Paul's message, and some of them became Christians.

One of the people Paul met was Lydia—a cloth merchant from Thyatira, a city in the province of Asia which Paul had been unable to visit himself. Now she would be the one to go back there and tell others about Jesus.

▲ Philippi
Even these ruins show that Philippi must have been a sophisticated and elegant city in Roman times. It was a Roman "colony"—a place where government officials and high-ranking soldiers could enjoy a comfortable retirement.

PRISONERS

Day after day, as Paul and his friends tried to tell the people of Philippi about Jesus, they were followed by a woman who shouted against them.

She was a slave who told fortunes. This made a lot of money for her owners. But Paul could see that she was really ill and they were just taking advantage of her. He healed her in the name of Jesus.

Her owners were furious because she no longer wanted to tell fortunes. Ignoring the laws that protected Roman citizens, they had Paul and Silas dragged before the authorities, whipped, and thrown into jail. In a cell with their feet held fast between heavy blocks of wood, Paul and Silas couldn't sleep. At midnight they were awake praying to God and singing hymns.

Suddenly they felt the shock of an earthquake. The prison doors opened, and their chains fell off.

The jailer awoke. He saw the prison doors open and panicked. Certain he would be put to death for letting the prisoners escape, he reached for his sword.... But Paul cried out, "Don't harm yourself, we're all here!"

Paul told him about Jesus, and the jailer became a Christian then and there, along with all his family.

Paul visits Athens

Athens was the cultural center of the Roman Empire. Centuries before, it had been home to great philosophers, and in Paul's time serious thinkers still liked to sit and debate all day long.

When Paul went there, he was surprised to see so many statues of gods and goddesses all over the city. There was even one "to the unknown god."

"This is the God I've come to tell you about," Paul said. He went on to tell them about Jesus, and a few of them became Christians.

▲ **A Greek temple**
These ruins are all that remain of a temple in Athens, built in honor of the goddess Athena. It was built 500 years before the time of Jesus.

Moving on

The authorities in Philippi soon discovered that they had broken the law in the way they treated Paul. Embarrassed, they asked him to leave the city. He and his friends went on to other Greek cities: Thessalonica, Berea, Athens, and Corinth. Paul stayed in Corinth for eighteen months. They spoke of Jesus in each place, and many more people became Christians.

9 A New Church

From Greece, Paul went back to Jerusalem and told the church there everything that was happening. After a short stay back in Antioch, he set off on his travels again. This time, he paid a quick return visit to the churches in south Galatia, before heading for Ephesus (see page 8), the capital city of the province of Asia.

Paul in Ephesus

In Ephesus, Paul joined his good friend Priscilla and her husband, Aquila. He'd first met them in Corinth. Like him they were tentmakers.

Many Jews lived in Ephesus. Paul spent three months talking with them in the synagogue, explaining his faith in Jesus. Some of them became Christians, but others took a stand against what Paul was doing.

They made him leave the synagogue, so he hired a lecture hall belonging to a Greek teacher called Tyrannus. Every day, from eleven in the morning until four in the afternoon, he held discussions there about the Christian faith. That was the hottest part of the day, when most people would take a siesta. But many people still wanted to hear what Paul had to say. Soon there was a growing church in the city.

People from all over the province of Asia often came to Ephesus. A lot of them became Christians there. When they went back home, they told others about Jesus, and so the message was spread.

THE RIOT

Ephesus was famous for its temple to the goddess Diana. Craftworkers made a lot of money by selling small silver images of the goddess. But because of what Paul and his friends were doing, so many people became Christians that fewer and fewer customers wanted to buy them.

One day Demetrius, a silversmith, stirred up a furious crowd, and there was a riot! Two of Paul's friends were dragged to the great open-air theater. The crowd stayed there shouting and screaming for hours, until the town clerk managed to calm them down.

When things were quiet, Paul called the Christians together and said good-bye, so he could continue on his travels and encourage new Christians in other towns. He went back to Greece first, and then set sail for Jerusalem.

▶ **The rioters' route**
Paul's companions may have been dragged by a mob of angry Ephesians along this colonnaded road. It leads from the former harbor to the Roman theater.

▶**Diana of Ephesus**
Ephesus was a proud city, with a long and famous history. It had a massive temple in honor of a goddess whom the Greeks called Artemis and the Romans called Diana. It was one of the largest buildings anywhere in the Roman Empire, and was one of the greatest wonders of the ancient world.

Inside there was an image of the goddess, which was said to have fallen from heaven. The whole city was obsessed with magic and superstition, but many people were attracted by what Paul was saying about Jesus.

10 Going to Church in the First Century

When people decided to follow Jesus, they naturally wanted to meet with others who were also Christians. Jews had always met every Sabbath in the synagogue, to read their Scriptures and to pray. Christians also met together to worship God and to encourage one another. Sunday became their special day, because that was the day on which Jesus rose from the dead. But they met at other times, too, whenever they got the chance. The groups they formed were called churches.

A body of people

For the first Christians, the church was not a building; it was people. Here is how Paul described it:

Just take a look at yourself for a moment. You have a beautiful strong body, but it's not the same as anyone else's, is it? Your nose isn't the same shape as your best friend's—and your eyes are different colors too. People come in all shapes and sizes. It would be a dull world if we were all the same. We wouldn't even be able to recognize one another!

If your body was all nose, then you wouldn't be able to walk or see. We need many different parts working smoothly to give us healthy bodies—arms, legs, eyes, head, ears, as well as other parts you can't even see. God's church is like that. Think of all the people in it. They are different sizes and shapes, different colors— and they are all good at doing different things. Some are young, some are old, some are women, some are men. But nobody is more important than anyone else. In the church everyone is a very special person.

▲ **Roman Christians**
This Roman painting shows Christians "blessing the bread" as they meet together.

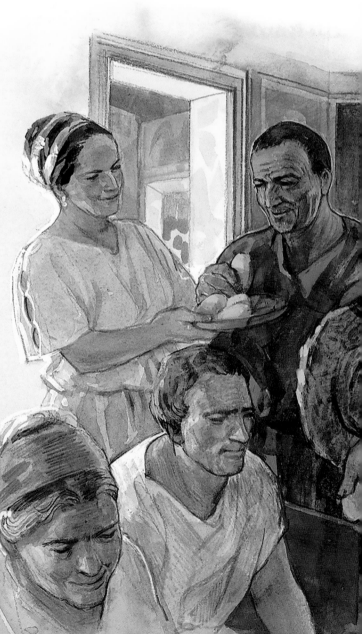

Meeting for worship

The first Christians met for worship in people's homes. After the day's work was done, they shared a meal with friends and talked about Jesus. It was more like a party than the kind of service that is held in many church buildings today.

People of all ages were there, and anyone could speak. Women, men, girls, boys, managers, workers, and slaves were all of equal value in the church.

Someone might sing a hymn of praise to God. Another might speak of what Jesus had taught. Others might pray aloud, or bring a special message that God had given them.

While they were eating their meal together, they would share bread and wine as Jesus had done just before He was crucified.

People who were not yet Christians would be there, too, and those who loved Jesus would always talk about Him, and tell the others how the Spirit of Jesus had changed their lives.

Spiritual gifts

The early church had a place for everyone, and many New Testament passages refer to the different kinds of skills which Christians had. They are sometimes called "spiritual gifts" or, more accurately, "charismatic gifts," from the Greek word *charismata*, meaning "the gifts of God's grace." They could include activities such as the ability to teach other people about Jesus, or being able to pray in ways that were especially helpful to others. But they also included more unusual things, like the power of healing the sick, or of speaking in strange languages ("speaking in tongues"). These and many other "spiritual gifts" were highly valued because they showed that the Christian message speaks to the whole person—bodies and spirits as well as minds.

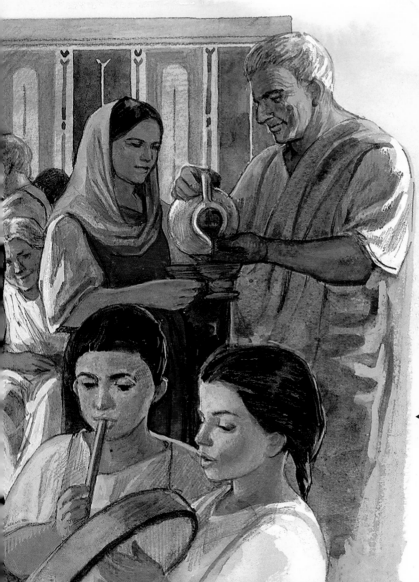

An ancient hymn in praise of Jesus

God came to earth as a human—
Jesus Christ.
God's Spirit—and the angels—
gave their support
to show that His message was true.
The good news was taken to every nation,
people all over the world believed in Him,
and He returned in glory to heaven.

◀ A church meeting
Most Christian meetings took place in Roman-style villas. These were large buildings, home not just to the people who owned them, but to all their workers too.

11 Keeping in Touch

Paul never stayed in one place for long. He wanted to share the good news about Jesus with as many people as he could. But the new Christians had lots of questions. To answer them, Paul wrote letters.

Writing letters

When people write a letter nowadays, they usually put the date first, then their address, then the name of the person they are writing to. They usually begin "Dear—." At the end, they sign off with "Love" to a friend, or "Yours sincerely" to someone they don't know very well.

Archaeologists have found many letters from Paul's day. By comparing Paul's letters with others they have found, they can tell that Paul was sending very personal letters to people he knew and loved well—the sort of letter that children might write to their parents, or lovers would write to one another.

Did you know?

Paul's handwriting was large and untidy, which made it easy to recognize but hard to read. He had poor eyesight, which didn't help. This probably explains why his letters were always written down by a secretary from his dictation.

▲ A Roman pencil case
Reed pens were kept in one compartment, and a cake of ink in the other. The reed pens had to be "sharpened" like a present-day pencil to keep a good point on the nib—so they grew shorter and shorter until they were too small to use!

Paul's letters

Paul dictated his letters to a secretary. The letters almost always follow the same pattern.

Paul's own name comes first, followed by the name of the people he is writing to.

Then comes a greeting, usually "peace and grace."

Thanksgiving generally comes next—a prayer in which Paul gives thanks to God for the people he is writing to.

After that, he gets down to the questions he has been asked, and advises his readers about how to live for Jesus.

He then adds personal greetings to individuals and gives news about other people they know.

Paul writes a short note in his own handwriting, to guarantee that the letter is really from him.

He ends with a sentence of farewell and blessing.

▲ Letters
Letters in New Testament times were written on papyrus, which was made from layering thin strips of the stems of the papyrus reed and applying pressure to the layers. The natural juice in the stem acted like glue.

Living the Christian faith

Most of Paul's letters were written to answer Christians' questions about how to live. In the letters he wrote to the Christians at Corinth, in Greece, he answered many different questions.

Was it right to eat food from pagan temples—food that had been offered to other gods?

Paul said that it was right, but it might offend some Christians. Those Christians who had no problem buying and eating the food must take care not to upset others in this way.

Should Christians get married?

Yes, said Paul, people who wanted to marry should do so, even though he was not married himself.

Were some Christian leaders more important than others?

No, said Paul, they were all just doing God's work.

Should Christians' lifestyles be different from other people's?

Yes, said Paul. People should be able to see that believing in Jesus really does make a difference to the way people behave.

Should a Christian expect to be rich and famous?

No, said Paul. He had been thrown into prison many times, and Jesus Himself had been rejected and crucified. Following and serving Jesus might often lead to suffering.

12 Paul in Jerusalem

Paul knew he must visit Rome. It was the capital of the Empire, and many Christians lived there. He could easily have gone direct from Greece to Italy on his third journey. But it seems that while he was in Greece, he simply wrote a letter to prepare the way for a later visit and to encourage the Christian group in Rome in their faith.

The letter to Rome

Many Christians in Rome wanted to know if Paul really had given up believing in the Hebrew Scriptures, as some of his enemies claimed. Paul's letter to them told them what he really believed. He repeated many of the same arguments he had included in an earlier letter to Christians in Galatia —that he loved his own Jewish people, and that belief in Jesus was not a denial of the Jewish faith, but was really what all their ancestors had been looking forward to. He was not rejecting the Jewish faith by believing in Jesus. Rather, Jesus was the Messiah the Jews were hoping for.

A gift for Jerusalem

Before going to Rome, Paul was eager to visit the Jewish Christians in Jerusalem. He wanted to reassure them that many non-Jewish Christians in Greece and Asia loved Jesus just as much as they did. He came up with a brilliant idea. The Christians in Jerusalem had always been quite poor, and Paul asked the Gentile churches to take a collection to send as a gift.

Though many were poor, they gave very generously, and soon Paul was on his way to Palestine, along with some of his Gentile Christian friends.

When his ship docked in the port of Caesarea, he and his companions stayed in the home of Philip. While they were there, a prophet with special insight from God brought them a message, telling Paul that he would be taken prisoner when he got to Jerusalem. But Paul knew he must still go on.

When he arrived, the church leaders gave him a warm welcome. They suggested that if he went to the temple to worship God, even his enemies would realize that he was still a faithful Jew himself and everything would be all right.

THE ANGRY MOB

The Christians in Jerusalem had a plan for Paul. Four of their number were going to make a special offering in the temple. They wanted Paul to go with them.

"If you go and pay their expenses," the church leaders said, "then people will see you are not really against the Jewish faith."

It seemed a good idea, so Paul and the four Jewish Christians went to the temple. But trouble was not far off. Some Jewish visitors from Ephesus had seen Paul in the street with Trophimus, a Gentile Christian.

"We knew Paul wasn't to be trusted," they said.

"Look at him—he's taking a Gentile into our very own temple, although it is forbidden. We have to get rid of him once and for all."

When they heard that, the crowds were really angry. They wanted Paul dead. They seized him and dragged him out of the temple and started beating him.

Things were looking ugly.

"Call the troops," someone said. And the Roman commander rushed down to the scene of the riot with some soldiers. They grabbed Paul, clapped him in chains, and marched him off to the fort.

When the commander heard Paul speak eloquent Greek, he knew he was not just a gangster. And when Paul told him he was a Roman citizen, the commander knew it was his duty to protect him from the mob.

So Paul was arrested—for his own safety.

◄ **The fort of Antonia**
The soldiers had to carry Paul into the fort of Antonia, their base near the temple in Jerusalem, because the mob had become so wild.

▲ **The rules of the temple**
The Greek words on this inscription from Herod's temple say that no Gentiles may cross the barrier to the inner courts on pain of death. Paul was suspected of encouraging his friends to break the rules.

13 On the Way to Rome

From the time of his arrest in Jerusalem, Paul was never free again. He lived the rest of his life as a prisoner.

On trial

Paul was brought before the Jewish Council to be tried. When he told them about his faith in Jesus as the Messiah of the Jewish people, they could not agree what to do next. Some of them wanted to believe what Paul was saying, but others wanted him put to death.

There was a plot to have Paul killed secretly. But the Roman commander heard of it, and took him to Caesarea for safety. Felix, the Roman governor, lived there. Paul was called before his court, but Felix was not really interested and left Paul in prison. He had some freedom, and was allowed to see his friends.

Appeal to Caesar

The governor Felix left Paul in prison for two years without giving him a proper trial. Then another governor was appointed: Porcius Festus. Paul was fed up, and wanted to move on to Rome. Any Roman citizen had the right to be heard by the Emperor, so when Festus called for him, Paul asked him to send his case to the Emperor's court right away.

Festus could not refuse this request, but he had no idea what to write in his report to Emperor Nero. He knew nothing about the Jewish religion and couldn't understand what all the fuss was about.

▼ The long way to Rome
Paul and his fellow travelers were blown miles off course by an autumn storm and the ship was eventually wrecked on a sandbar in what is now St. Paul's Bay, Malta.

Just then, the local Jewish ruler—King Herod Agrippa—and his wife visited Caesarea. They knew about such things, and Festus asked for their advice.

The three of them listened as Paul told them of the great light on the road to Damascus all those years before, and of all the wonderful things that had happened as a result of his meeting with Jesus. They were impressed. In fact, Agrippa said, "You are almost persuading me to become a Christian."

They agreed that Paul had done nothing illegal. But he had already appealed to Rome, and there was no going back on that.

THE SHIPWRECK

It was late September when Paul and his friends set sail from Caesarea to Rome. They made slow progress around the coast until they came to Myra. There, they were put on a ship that was bound for Italy.

They sailed to a harbor on the island of Crete. But it was now well into autumn, and it seemed unwise to travel farther, as winter storms could be dangerous.

However, a gentle wind from the south began to blow, and the sailors thought they could easily take the boat to a better harbor farther up the coast. No sooner had they set sail than a very strong wind—a "North-easter"—blew down from the island, and the ship was carried off course.

The men took down the sail and let the ship run before the wind. The next day they threw some of the cargo overboard to lighten the ship. For fourteen days the storm raged, and they could see neither sun by day nor stars by night.

"Don't worry," Paul reassured them. "It's true the ship will be lost. But God will save all our lives."

That night, the sailors suspected that they were close to land. Afraid of smashing on the rocks, they put out all their anchors to hold the ship steady for a while. Paul encouraged everyone to have some food, to give themselves strength.

In the morning, they saw land. They cut the ship free from its anchors and tried to steer it to shore. But the ship ran aground on a sandbank, and everyone had to swim for their lives, holding on to planks or broken pieces of the ship to keep them afloat.

Somehow, everyone made it. They were on the island of Malta, and they stayed there until winter was over and they could set sail again.

When Paul arrived in Rome, many Christians came to welcome him. His trial was delayed and he had two years in which to tell all he could about Jesus.

▼ **St. Paul's Bay**
A view of the bay where Paul and his fellow travelers scrambled ashore when their ship was wrecked.

14 A Prisoner in Rome

Paul's "prison" in Rome was not a dungeon, but a house he rented for himself, with soldiers to guard him.

Many Christians visited him there. He also received news from churches in other places, and wrote letters to encourage and advise them.

Paul's letter to Philippi

The church at Philippi in northern Greece was one of Paul's favorites. He was very moved when they sent him a gift of money—he knew then that they really cared about him. The money helped to pay his expenses. Not only did he have to buy his own food and pay rent for the house he stayed in—he also had to pay the wages of the soldiers who were guarding him!

In his letter, Paul thanked the Christians in Philippi for their generosity, and also encouraged them to keep trusting in Jesus. He knew that he could have been much richer if he had not spent his life sharing the message about Jesus.

"But," he wrote, "what I have now is far more valuable than all I have lost. Knowing Jesus Christ as a friend is the most important thing in the whole world."

The runaway returns

Paul's letter to Colossae was carried there by Onesimus, a runaway slave who had become a Christian when he met Paul.

Paul also wrote a short letter to Onesimus' master, Philemon, asking him to welcome Onesimus back as a fellow Christian—no small thing, since the law allowed a master to put a runaway slave to death.

▲ **Colossae**
The ancient town of Colossae was set in a beautiful valley backed by mountains, in the west of present-day Turkey.

Paul's letter to Colossae

Colossae was a town in Asia Minor, east of Ephesus, and the home of a man named Epaphras. He had become a Christian as a result of meeting Paul in Ephesus, and on his return home he had told his friends about his new faith. Many of them became Christians, too, and soon there was a growing church in Colossae.

But the Christians there had questions. Who was Jesus really? Some thought He must be an angel, to be worshiped along with other gods and goddesses. Others were saying that to be really good Christians, they needed to carry out various ritual practices.

Paul wrote a letter to them from Rome. He said that Jesus truly was God, and believing in Him was the only thing that could make a person a Christian.

▲ **A slave badge**
This Roman slave badge says "Seize me if I should try to escape and send me back to my master on the estate of Callistus."

The death of Paul

No one knows for certain if Paul ever appeared at the Emperor's court. Some ancient traditions say he was released and went off on his travels again, this time to Spain. He was certainly beheaded in Rome during Emperor Nero's persecution of the Christians, and it is quite likely that he stayed in Rome from the time of his imprisonment until then.

15 The Christians in Rome

Rome was the capital of the Roman Empire, and had good links by road and sea with every part of it. It is hardly surprising that the news about Christianity reached Rome early on, although no one knows for sure who was the first to take the message there. It may even have been pilgrims from Rome who had gone to Jerusalem for the Pentecost festival and heard Peter preach!

Persecution

For a number of years, Christians in Rome and throughout the Empire were allowed to practice their religion openly. But some emperors took a definite dislike to the Christians. Nero, who ruled from 54–68 B.C. was one of these, and toward the end of his reign he persecuted the Christians in Rome with great cruelty.

Nero was probably mad, and the tortures he inflicted on Christians were terrible. He put some in the ring to fight wild animals, and charged people money to go and watch. Others he dipped in tar, and set them on fire to serve as torches to illuminate the driveway to his own palace.

Toward the end of the first century, Emperor Domitian (81–96 B.C.) attacked the Christians so violently that some wondered if he could be Nero come back to life again.

▲ Persecutors
These coins show the heads of the two Emperors who treated Christians the most cruelly: Nero and Domitian.

God and the emperor

The problem with the Christians was that they refused to worship the Roman Emperor. To them, he was only a human. But to the Romans, failing to worship the Emperor was like not paying taxes, or plotting to overthrow the state.

Besides, all sorts of other religions managed to include Emperor worship. The authorities could not see why Christians could not worship both Jesus and the Emperor.

It was not that simple. Christians were happy to obey laws about taxes and so on, but they knew that if Jesus was truly God, then He was the only one they should worship.

▶**Divine Augustus**
This Latin inscription found at Ephesus refers to the Emperor Augustus as "divine."

16 Apostles and Missionaries

Paul was not the only Christian who spent his life spreading the message of Jesus.

Paul and his friends

Paul achieved a lot, but he could never have done it without help from many others who worked with him.

Barnabas was a native of Cyprus. He persuaded the church in Antioch to invite Paul to help them, then later went with Paul on his first trip to Asia Minor.

Silas belonged to the Jerusalem church, and was a Roman citizen. He went with Paul on some of his travels and helped him to write the letters to Christians in Thessalonica (1 and 2 Thessalonians). He later worked with Peter.

Priscilla and Aquila were wife and husband, tentmakers like Paul, who traveled to many different cities sharing their faith.

Andronicus and Junia were another two apostles who were husband and wife. Women and men often worked together in the earliest churches.

Phoebe was a leader in the church at Corinth. She took letters from there to Paul while he was in Ephesus, and later carried his letter to the church in Rome.

Titus and Timothy helped Paul in Ephesus. Titus, a Gentile, visited Corinth as Paul's personal messenger at that time and later settled in Crete. Timothy was born in Lystra. His mother was Jewish and his father Greek. Paul regarded him as a special friend—almost a son to him, in fact—because Timothy gave him so much personal support.

Luke was a Gentile doctor. He stayed with Paul the whole time he was in prison in Caesarea and Rome, and he later wrote an account of the life of Jesus and another of the beginning of the church, including his own experiences with Paul. These two books are in the New Testament: the gospel of Luke and the Acts of the Apostles.

▼ **The encouragement of friends**
Fellow tentmakers Priscilla and Aquila encouraged Paul in his work of spreading the news about Jesus. They also traveled around spreading the news.

The church in Jerusalem

Jesus' disciples were the first leaders of the Jerusalem church. But some of them were killed, and others had to leave for their own safety.

In a short time, James was the church's leader. He was Jesus' brother but did not become a disciple until after Jesus' death and resurrection.

James strictly kept all the Jewish customs. It was said that his knees were like a camel's from all the praying he did! This is the James whom Paul met to try to decide if Gentile Christians should keep the Jewish laws.

In 62 B.C. James was killed for his faith. Not long after, a fierce war broke out between Jews and Romans. By 70 B.C. Jerusalem had been destroyed. The Jewish church grew smaller, and by the end of the century it had almost entirely disappeared.

Apostles
The term "apostle" comes from a Greek word that means "someone who is sent with a message." Jesus' twelve disciples had this title, but so did Paul, Barnabas, and many others. Jesus taught that everyone is special to God, and His first followers never forgot that.

◀ **The destruction of Jerusalem**
Treasures from the temple in Jerusalem were carried off to Rome after the Jews were defeated in their war with the Romans. Here, on the triumphal arch of the victorious Emperor Titus in Rome, is the seven-branched lampstand that stood in the Holy Place, which only the priests could enter.

▼ **The death of Peter**
When Jesus was arrested, Peter ran away and said he didn't know the Man. Years later, he let himself be put to death rather than give up his belief in Jesus.

Did you know?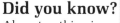
Almost nothing is known about what happened to Jesus' special disciples. Like Paul, Peter traveled a lot. He was married, and he worked with his wife telling people about Jesus. He eventually died in Rome during Nero's persecution—he was crucified upside down.

John also spread the message of Jesus. But his brother James was put to death not long after the martyrdom of Stephen. Judas killed himself after betraying Jesus.

More Letters and Their Writers

Paul was not the only person to write letters to churches which asked for his advice and assistance. Other Christian leaders also found this was an easy way to keep in touch with their churches.

A letter from James

The letter of James is one of the shortest New Testament books. It gives lots of advice on how Christians should behave.

The letter itself does not say who James was. He may have been the James who was the brother of Jesus, and leader of the church in Jerusalem. In some places the letter of James is quite similar to the teaching of Jesus, and has many illustrations taken from farming life in Palestine, such as those quoted on this page.

◄ **A warning from James:** "Rich people shouldn't trust in their money. You know how the hot sun shrivels wildflowers, and the petals all drop off leaving an ugly stalk. In the same way the rich will find they can lose everything as they go about their business."

Hebrews

Hebrews is not a letter, and no one knows who wrote it. It is more like a sermon or an essay, and was probably written to Jewish Christians living in Rome during Nero's time of persecution. Maybe they were trying to avoid suffering by still following the Jewish faith, and pretending they were not real Christians. The writer digs deep into the Hebrew Scriptures to tell them that by doing that they were letting down other Christians, and maybe even being disloyal to their faith.

A letter from Peter

Two letters have Peter's name on them, and are called 1 and 2 Peter. The first one was written to encourage Christians at a time of persecution.

"The Devil is your enemy," Peter wrote, "roaming around like a wild lion, looking for someone to eat." Maybe Peter was writing at the time when Nero was actually feeding Christians to the lions! But he encouraged his readers still to be courageous in sharing their faith.

"God will give you strength to endure," he said. "Remember how Jesus suffered for you, and be ready to follow His example."

▲ **A wild lion.** Peter warned Christians that they would face many dangers, as terrifying as facing a hungry lion.

Organizing the church

As time passed, the church grew bigger, and it needed to be more organized. The letters to Timothy and Titus contain instructions for the appointment of Christian leaders, and advice on how they should behave.

> A church leader should be married only once, should be generous and kind, a good teacher, and not the sort of person who likes to start a fight.

▼ Wise words from James
"The tongue is a very small thing, but it can make a big noise. It only takes a spark to light a huge bush fire. And it only takes one wrong word to start a big argument that can soon get out of control."

▼ A sharp reminder from James
"You must never treat people in different ways depending on how they dress. Imagine two people coming into your meeting. One is rich and has fine clothes and gold rings, and the other is a poor person dressed in rags. If you give the rich one a good seat, but you make the poor one sit on the floor, then you are not living as followers of Jesus should."

18 False Teachers and Troublemakers

No two churches were the same. The church in Corinth was different from the church in Philippi, and both of them were different from the churches in Ephesus and Jerusalem. The message of Jesus needed to be expressed in ways that different people could understand. That was never a problem until some Christians began asking what was really worth believing about Jesus.

◄ False teachers
A Christian named Jude said that teachers who caused divisions among Christians were like uprooted trees: They would never bear fruit; and would bring about their own destruction.

Is Jesus God?

One big question was about Jesus Himself. Who was He? Was He just another Jewish religious teacher, or was He God in person? From the very beginning, the Christians had always believed that Jesus really and truly was God.

But others were less sure. They wondered how God could possibly have been born to a human mother. In the Roman Empire, children were of little value until they grew up and could work. The idea that Jesus could have been God as a child did not appeal to them. Maybe Jesus had only *seemed* to be a real person. Or perhaps God only came into Jesus when He was baptized.

And how could God have died on the cross? Surely, they reasoned, God must have left Jesus before the crucifixion.

Arguments like this went on for many centuries before the church as a whole found satisfactory explanations. Meanwhile, John and others worked hard to guide people as they tried to follow Jesus, even though there were hard questions to face.

The letters of John

Toward the end of the first century, the three letters of John were written to deal with difficult questions, such as whether or not Jesus was God. The letter known as 1 John is the longest of them. It was written to a church which had been torn apart by fierce debates about all this. Some people had left the church altogether and started a rival group. They believed God had given them special knowledge that the others didn't have, and which gave them a more advanced form of faith than the rest. John's advice was simple:

▶ "People who follow Jesus should behave as Jesus did. They must love God, and love other people."

▶ "Anyone who believes that Jesus was God come as a human being has the spirit of God in them. Anyone who denies this does not belong to God."

Jude and 2 Peter

These short letters were written to people who were arguing about the same matters as the church John knew. False (heretical) teachers of all kinds were trying to take the church over for themselves, and get people to accept their own point of view. Jude and 2 Peter both tell their readers to stand by what the first followers of Jesus believed, and not allow themselves to be turned away from what is true.

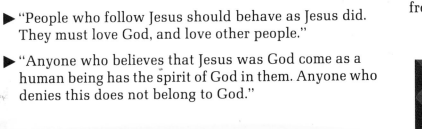

John

The letters of John are very similar to the Gospel of John. They must have been written by the same person. Ancient tradition says this was John, one of Jesus' first disciples, and that after working in Palestine his life ended as an old man in Ephesus.

 Kind words from John

Dear friends, let us love one another, because love comes from God. Whoever loves is a child of God and knows God. Whoever does not love does not know God, for God is love. And God's love is shown by the fact that God's Son came into the world, so that we might have life through Him.

19 Hope for the Future

Before Jesus left His disciples, He promised that He would return again at the end of time. The early Christians always believed that.

Questions from Thessalonica

When Paul visited Thessalonica in Greece, many people became Christians. Paul told them that Jesus would return and put right all that was wrong in the world. They were so excited that some of them gave up work, so that they could spend as much time as possible getting ready for Jesus' return. When it didn't happen, they wondered what to do next. Paul was concerned when he heard this and sent letters of advice.

Letters to Thessalonica

Paul's advice to the Thessalonians was straightforward: Christians should always be ready to meet Jesus whenever He might come back. But until then, they must live as good citizens. It was not a good idea to give up work and expect other people to feed and clothe them for nothing!

He also answered another question: What happens to Christians who die before Jesus returns? Do they miss out? No, said Paul, quite the opposite. They will be raised from death and will meet Jesus even before those who are still alive.

New heaven and new earth

The book called Revelation is the very last book in the New Testament. It was written at the end of the first century. Domitian was then Emperor, and the Christians were suffering great persecution because of their faith in Jesus.

Revelation was written by John, a Christian who had been sent to the prison island of Patmos in the Aegean Sea. The prisoners there were kept hard at work in the stone quarries during the day. As John looked around him, he asked some important questions.

▶**Prisoners at work**
Prisoners quarry stone on the island of Patmos. One of these prisoners wrote the book called Revelation.

If God is good, he wondered, why do so many innocent people suffer? Why does God not do something to stop all the injustice in the world? Why do evil people always seem to come out on top, while good people are oppressed?

John's answer came in visions of people, animals, and angels, which he describes in his book. Through it all he saw how God deals with the problem of evil. He learned that those who seem powerful do not always have the real power. Jesus was not a powerful person—He was crucified. But through His death the power of evil was defeated. God is concerned about justice, and in the end everything will be put right. Even powerful rulers like the Roman Emperors would one day be judged for the wrong they did.

There will be a new heaven and a new earth. God's home will be with the people. God will personally wipe away all their tears. There will be no more death, and no more crying or pain.

Did you know?
Revelation uses a kind of coded language, so that if the Romans read it they would not understand its message. The number 666 is used to stand for "Nero," and Rome itself is always called "Babylon."

▲ Patmos
A view of Patmos today. Perhaps this is what the writer of Revelation saw after a day's labor in the quarries.

Being a Christian

The first Christians had just one message: Wherever they went, they spoke about Jesus and His love for everyone.

◄ **A Christian symbol**
This Roman lamp is marked with two Greek letters—Chi and Rho—the first letters in the Greek word for Christ. The so-called "Chi-Rho" is still used as a Christian symbol.

Basic belief

In his message on the day of Pentecost, Peter said six things about being a Christian.

► The Hebrew Scriptures made many wonderful promises about how people could know God as a personal friend. Those promises had all come true through what Jesus said and did.

► When Jesus spoke, He brought a message from God. When He died on the cross He made it possible for all the wrong ever done in the world to be forgiven. And when He rose from death, everyone knew that He could be trusted, and what He had said was true.

► After His resurrection, Jesus returned to heaven. Out of love for this world and its people, God had come into an ordinary family as the child Jesus. No one could ever see God, but by looking at Jesus they could begin to understand what God is really like.

► Jesus promised that with His help, ordinary people would do extraordinary things. The power of God's Spirit was a gift for all those who believed in Him.

► God is concerned about all the injustice and wrong that is in the world. One day, it will all be put right and wrongdoers will be punished. Jesus will return to this earth as judge and ruler.

► People may choose whether or not to follow Jesus. Peter and the other apostles knew it would never be easy to believe in Him. It could lead to prison, even death. But they still believed it was worth following Jesus. His teachings helped them make sense of life, and they knew they could trust His promises.

▼ **Peter follows Jesus' example**
Shortly after he received the Holy Spirit at Pentecost, Peter healed a lame man in the temple. As he said in his speech, with Jesus' help ordinary people would do extraordinary things.

The stories about Jesus

As Paul and others took this message around the world, people wanted to know more about Jesus before they could decide whether to trust Him for themselves. The Christians told them of Jesus' great love for all people, and about His wonderful teachings.

At this time, there were no books about Jesus, so the stories were passed on by word of mouth. By the time there were Christians in many different parts of the Roman Empire it was necessary to write some of these things down. Different people wrote their own accounts. These are the Gospels of the New Testament: Matthew, Mark, Luke, and John.

Telling the message

Everyone needed to be able to understand the Christian message for themselves. When Paul was speaking with Jewish people, he told them Jesus was the Messiah they were looking for. Gentile people had different questions, and Paul spoke with them of the way God's presence can be seen all over the world. But he told everyone of how Jesus had died to put right all the world's wrongs, of the Holy Spirit who could help people to live in Jesus' way—and of the great honor of belonging to the church.

▼ Christian communities

Christianity grew throughout the Empire in spite of official opposition. This map shows Christian communities known to have existed by 325 B.C.

Rome

Mediterranean Sea

Jerusalem

There were Christians in these areas by the following dates:
- before Paul's travel
- by 100 CE
- by 185 CE
- by 325 CE

Finding Out More

If you want to know more about what you've read in *Wind and Fire*, you can look up the stories in the Bible.

The usual shorthand method has been used to refer to Bible passages. Each Bible book is split into chapters and verses. Take **1 Corinthians 13:1–12**, for example. This refers to Paul's first letter to the church at Corinth; chapter 13; verses 1 to 12.

1   Small Beginnings

Acts 12:1–11	**The start of the church**
Acts 16:11–15; 17:16–21; 1 Corinthians 1:26-27	**Spreading the message**
Acts 8:26–40	**Philip and the Ethiopian**

2   Wind and Fire

Matthew 27:3–8; Luke 24:45–49; John 20:19; Acts 1:8, 18–19	**Wind and Fire**
Leviticus 23:15–17	**Pentecost**
Joel 2:28–32; Acts 2:1–42	**A special Pentecost**
Acts 2:7–11	**Pilgrims from many places**
John 20:24–29; Acts 4:32–35	**The birthday of the church**

3   Danger Ahead

Acts 3:1–10; 12:12; 16:13	**Danger Ahead**
Acts 4:1–31; 5:20–42; 6:7	**Hard questions**
Acts 7:54–60	**A mob killing**
Acts 6:8—7:60	**A Christian is killed**
Acts 6:1–6	**Seven deacons**

4   The Persecutor

Acts 9:3–20	**On the road to Damascus**
Acts 7:54—8:1; 9:1–2	**Saul**
Acts 22:3	**Saul and his family**
Acts 22:24–29	**Roman citizens**

5   Peter Leads the Way

Acts 10:32; Galatians 3:28	**Peter Leads the Way**
Acts 10:4–48	**Peter's dream**
Acts 8:40	**Did you know?**

6   A Dangerous Journey

Acts 13:4—14:28	**Special instructions**
Acts 18:3	**A working preacher**
Acts 17:16–17	**Meeting people where they are**
Acts 15:1; Galatians 3:28	**Jews and Gentiles**

7   Jews and Gentiles

Acts 15:2	**Jewish and Gentile Christians**
Daniel 1:8–15	**Problems at a party**
Genesis 22:17–18; Exodus 20:1–10; Acts 22:3; Romans 4:1–25	**Paul and the big question**
Acts 15:4–32	**The meeting in Jerusalem**

8   A New Adventure

Acts 15:36–40	**A New Adventure**
Acts 16:9–15	**Paul visits Europe**
Acts 16:16–34	**Prisoners**
Acts 17:16–34	**Paul visits Athens**
Acts 17:1—18:11	**Moving on**

9   A New Church

Acts 18:22–23	**A New Church**
Acts 19:8–10	**Paul in Ephesus**
Acts 19:23–41; 20:1—21:14	**The riot**

10   Going to Church in the First Century

1 Corinthians 12:12–26	**A body of people**
1 Corinthians 11:23–26; 14:26–33	**Meeting for worship**
1 Corinthians 12:1–11	**Spiritual gifts**
1 Timothy 3:16	**An ancient hymn in praise of Jesus**

Index